I0454706

Fungi Fancy

COLORING BOOK

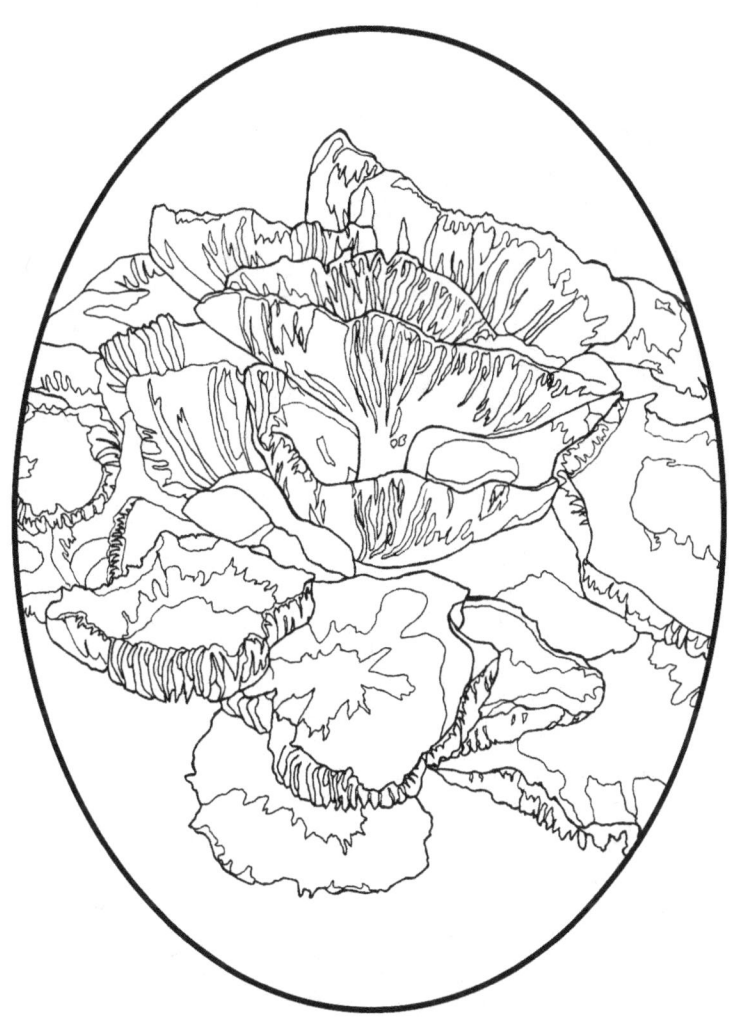

TWENTY-FOUR MUSHROOMS TO COLOR ANY WAY YOU LIKE

WWW.ALISONDNEVILLE.COM

ILLUSTRATED BY
ALISON NEVILLE

A SPECIAL THANKS GOES TO MY MOTHER, ROBIN NEVILLE, FOR PICKING ME UP OUT OF CREATIVE RUTS.
ALSO TO RAY AND MARY WILSON FOR HOMEMADE ARTIST RETREATS AND FORAYS. ANOTHER THANK YOU TO
MY FRIENDS THAT SNAPPED MUSHROOM PHOTOS FOR ME DURING THEIR TRAVELS-

JENESSA LINGARD

LARA MCALLISTER MCNAIR

CHRISTINE MOSS

ALEX WILLIAMS

OTHER TITLES INCLUDE: SACRED SLOTHS AND SULTRY SEA SLUGS

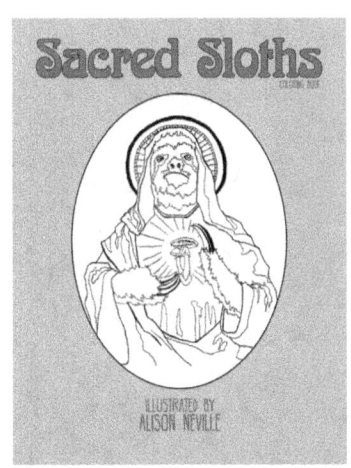

PUBLISHED 11/12/2016 BY CREATESPACE

©ALISON NEVILLE

ISBN-13: 978-1510385048

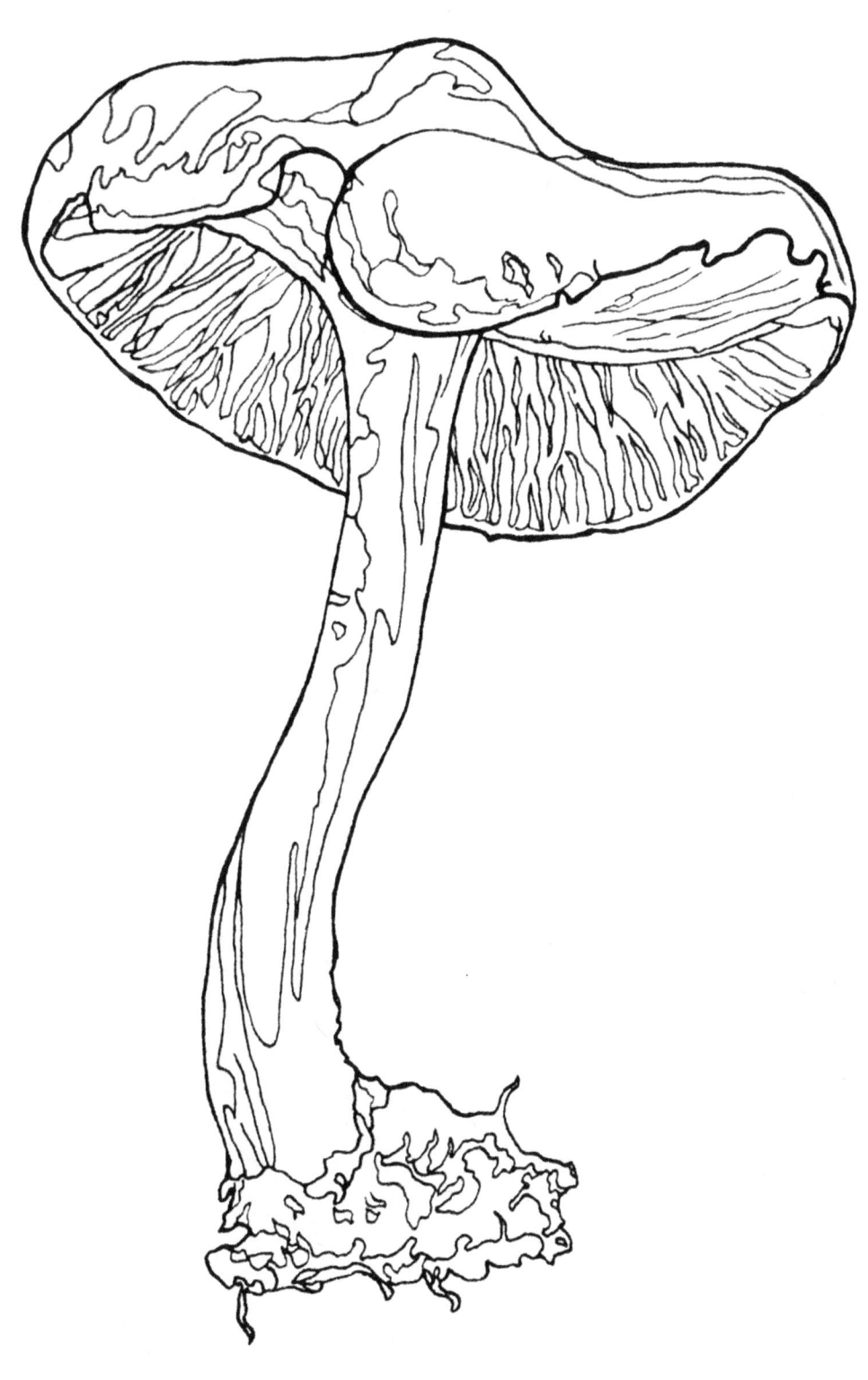

AGARICALES, SMALL BROWN MUSHROOM

RUBROBOLETUS SATANAS, SATAN'S BOLETE

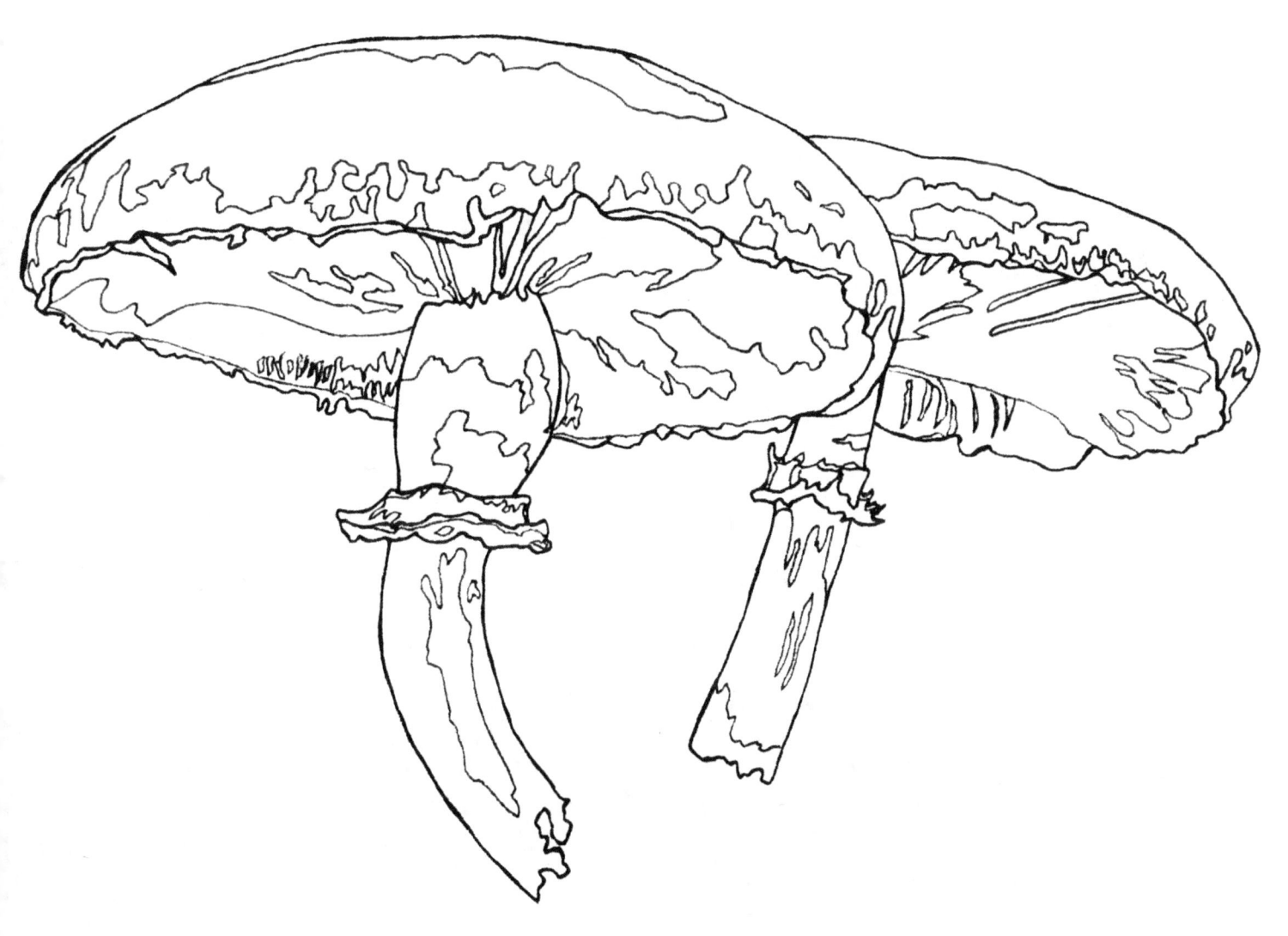

STROPHARIA RUGOSOANNULATA

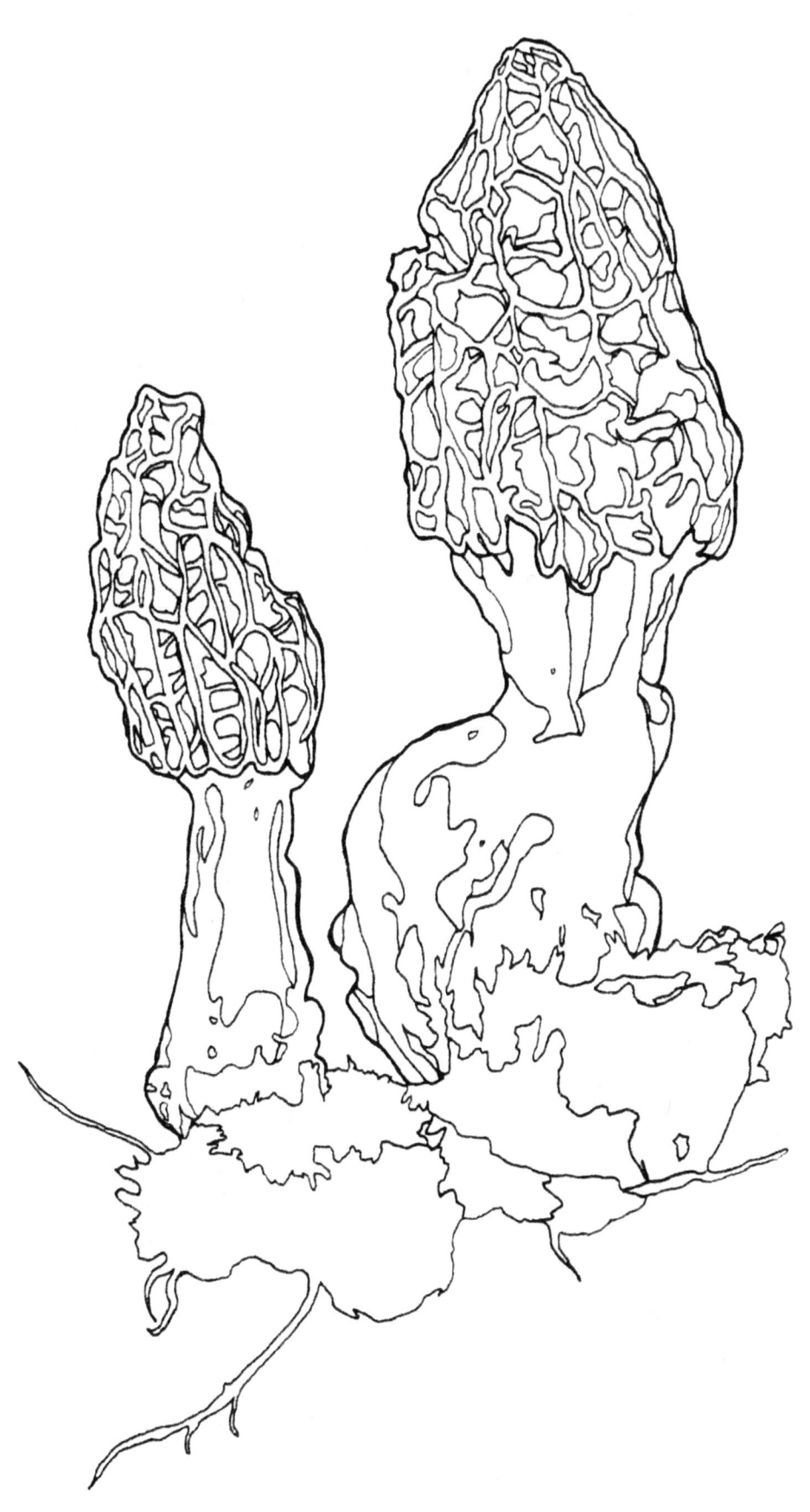

MORCHELLA SNYDERI, BLACK MOREL

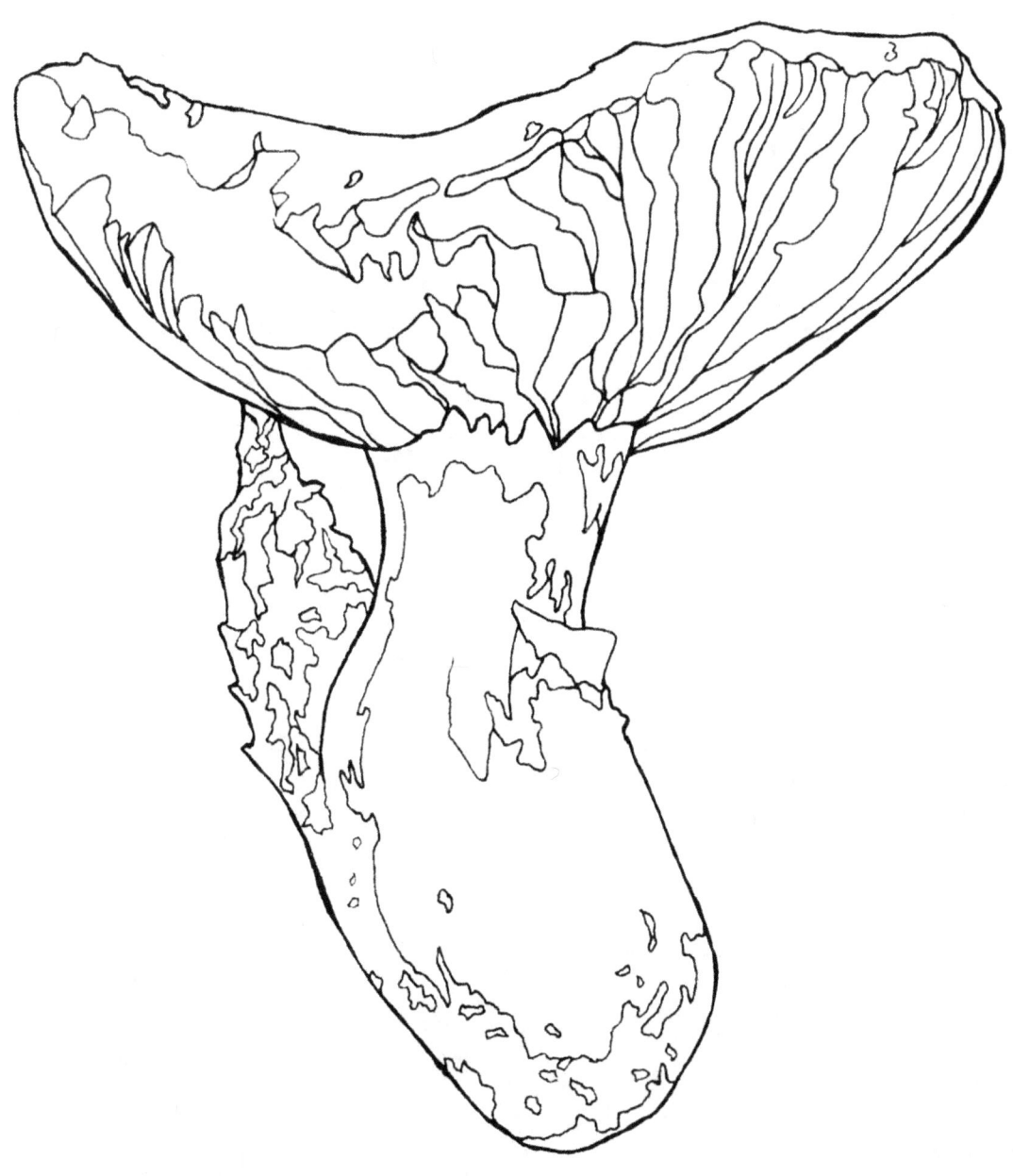

RUSSALA

PHALLUS IMPUDICUS, COMMON STINKHORN

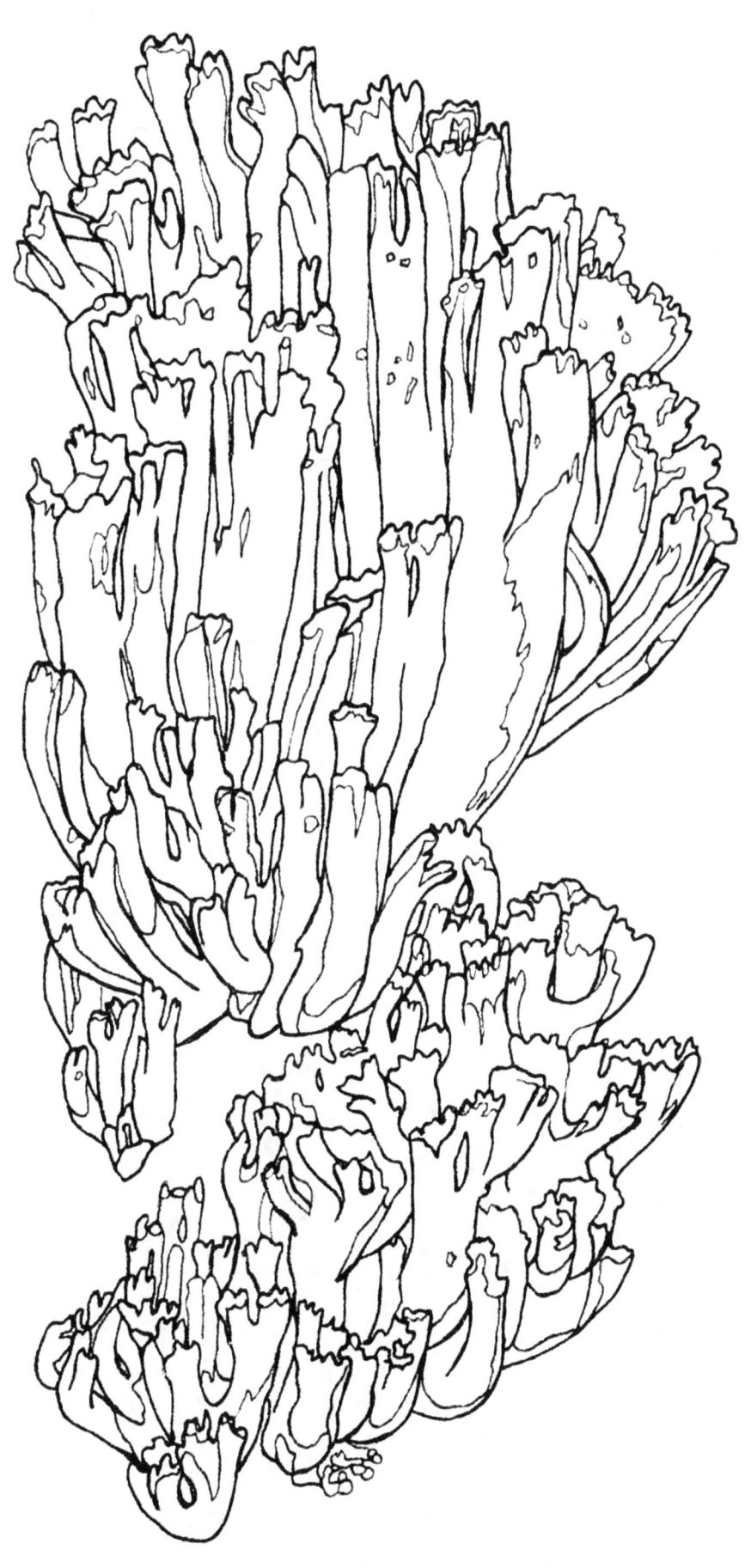

RAMARIA, CORAL FUNGUS

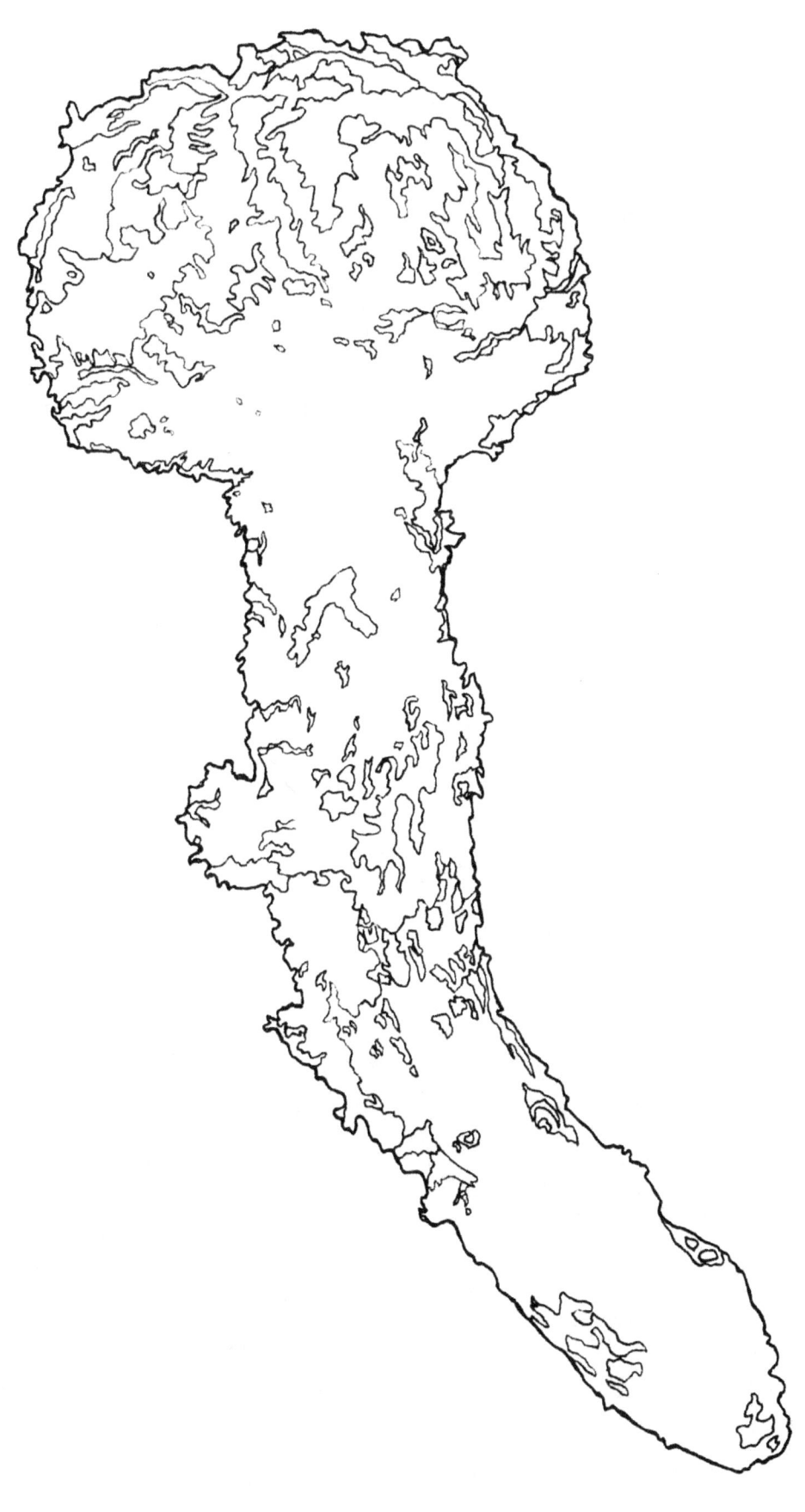

STROBILOMYCES STROBILACEUS, OLD MAN OF THE WOODS

ARMILLARIA SOLIDIPES

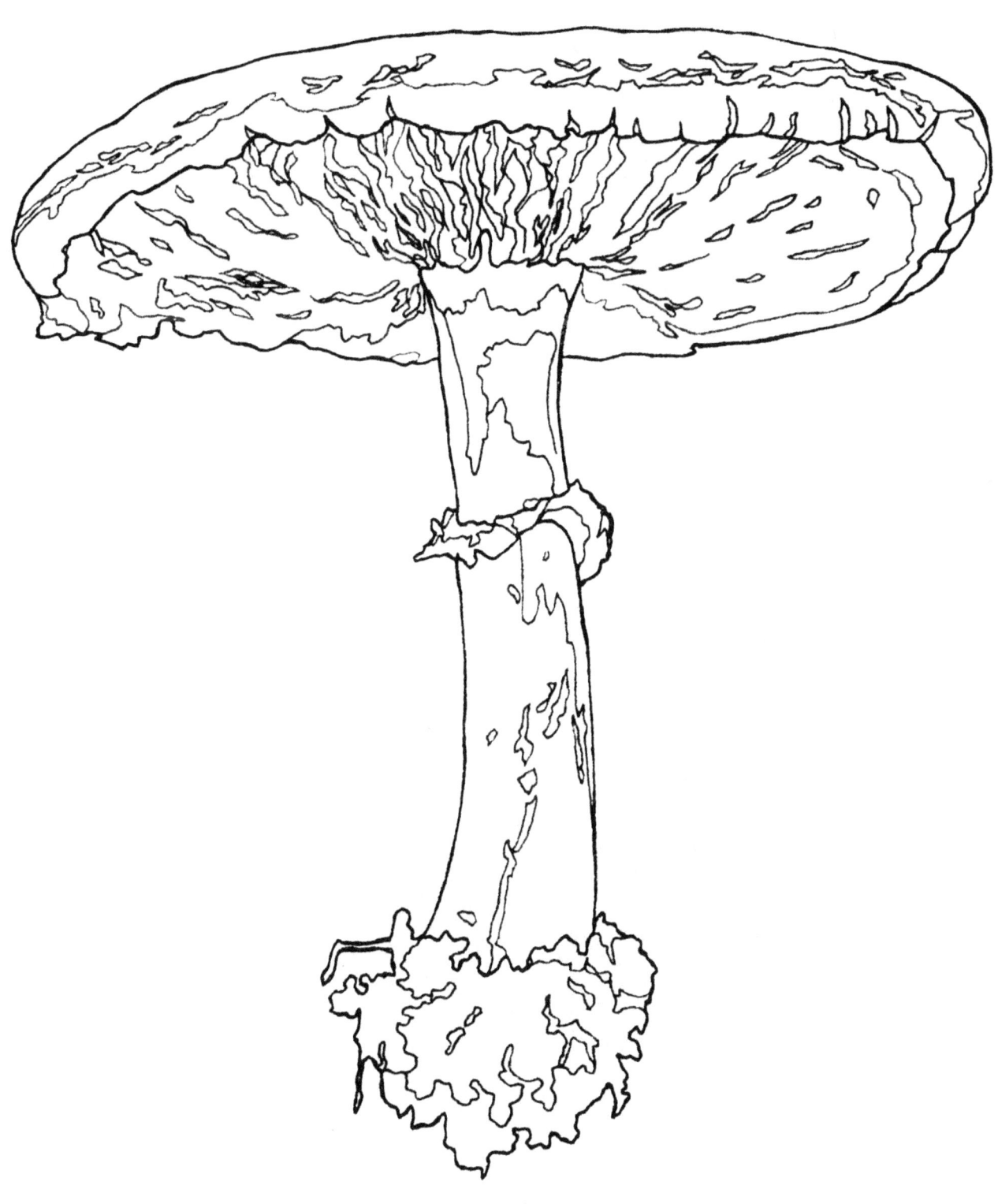

AGARICUS

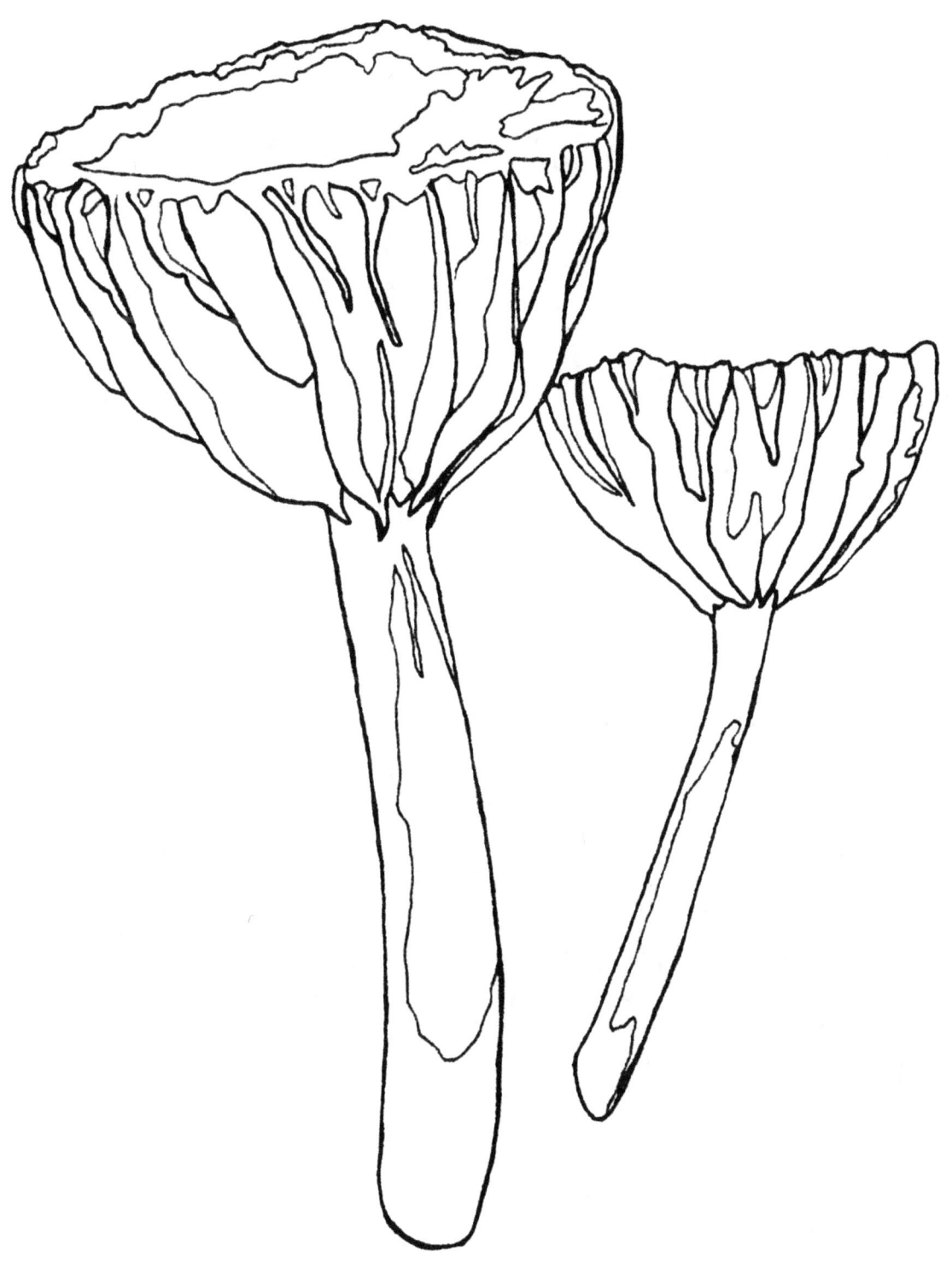

AGARICALES

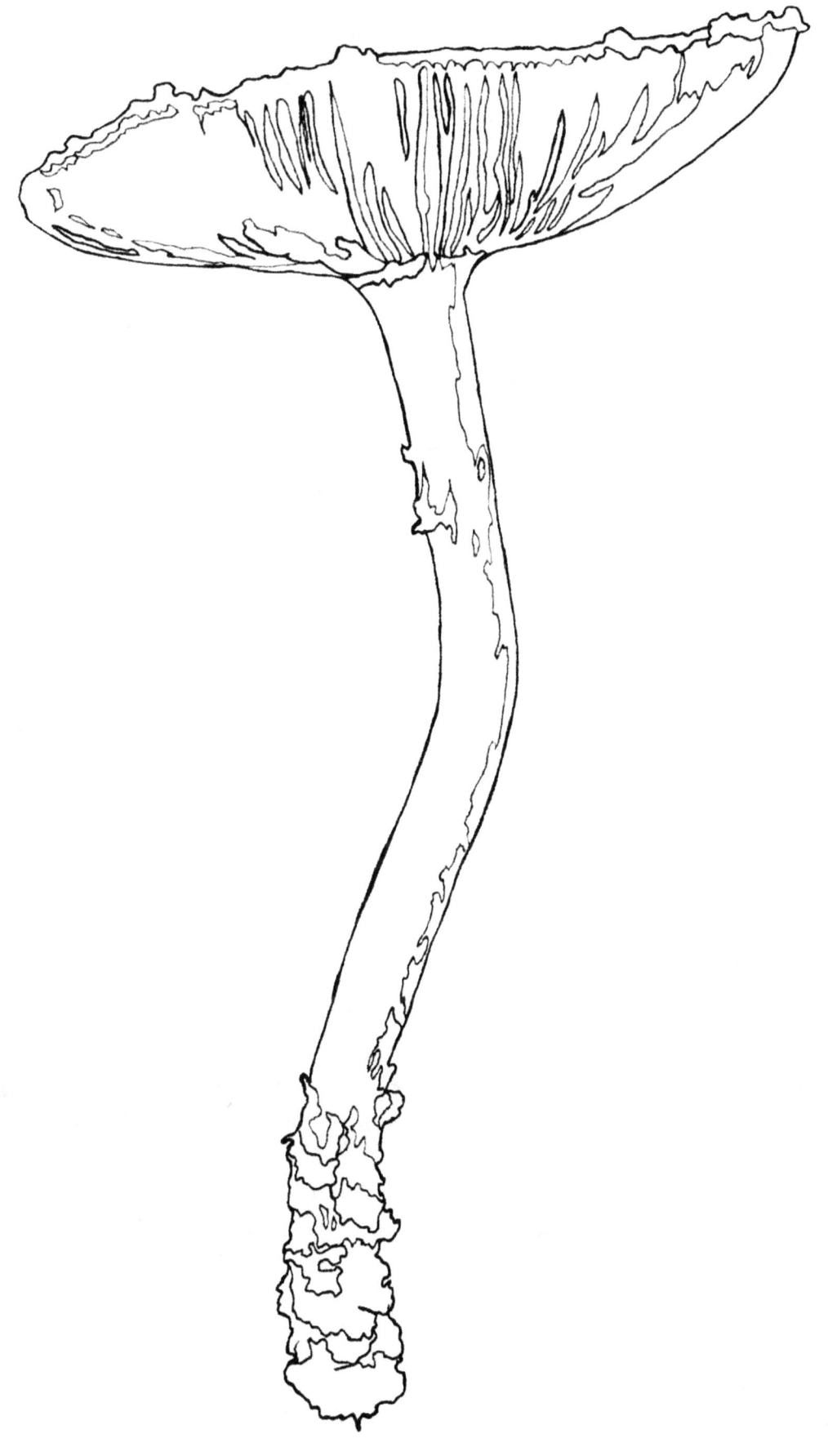

AMANITA ELONGATA

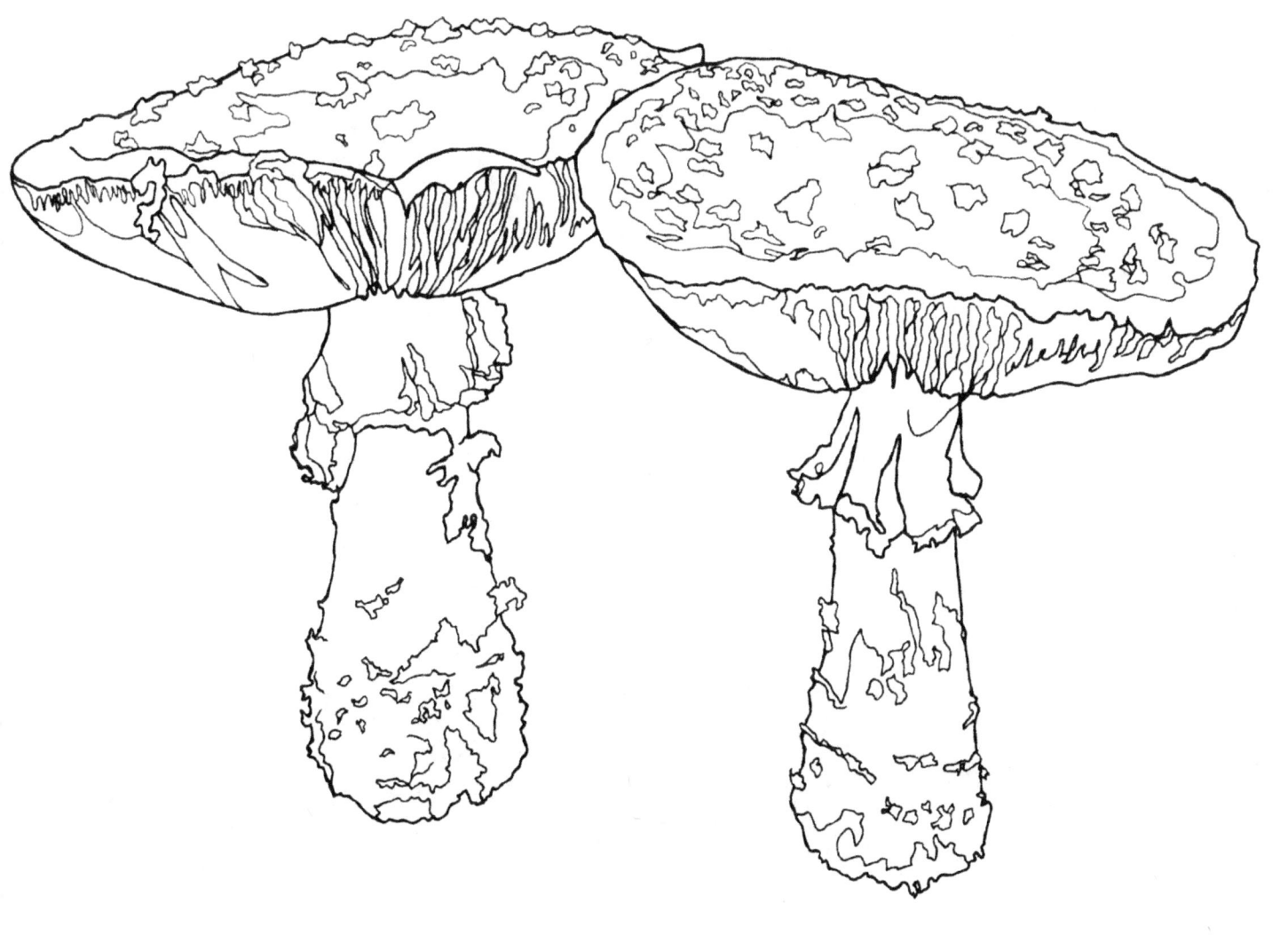

AMANITA MUSCARIA, FLY AGARIC

CLITOCYBE OR HYPSIZYGUS

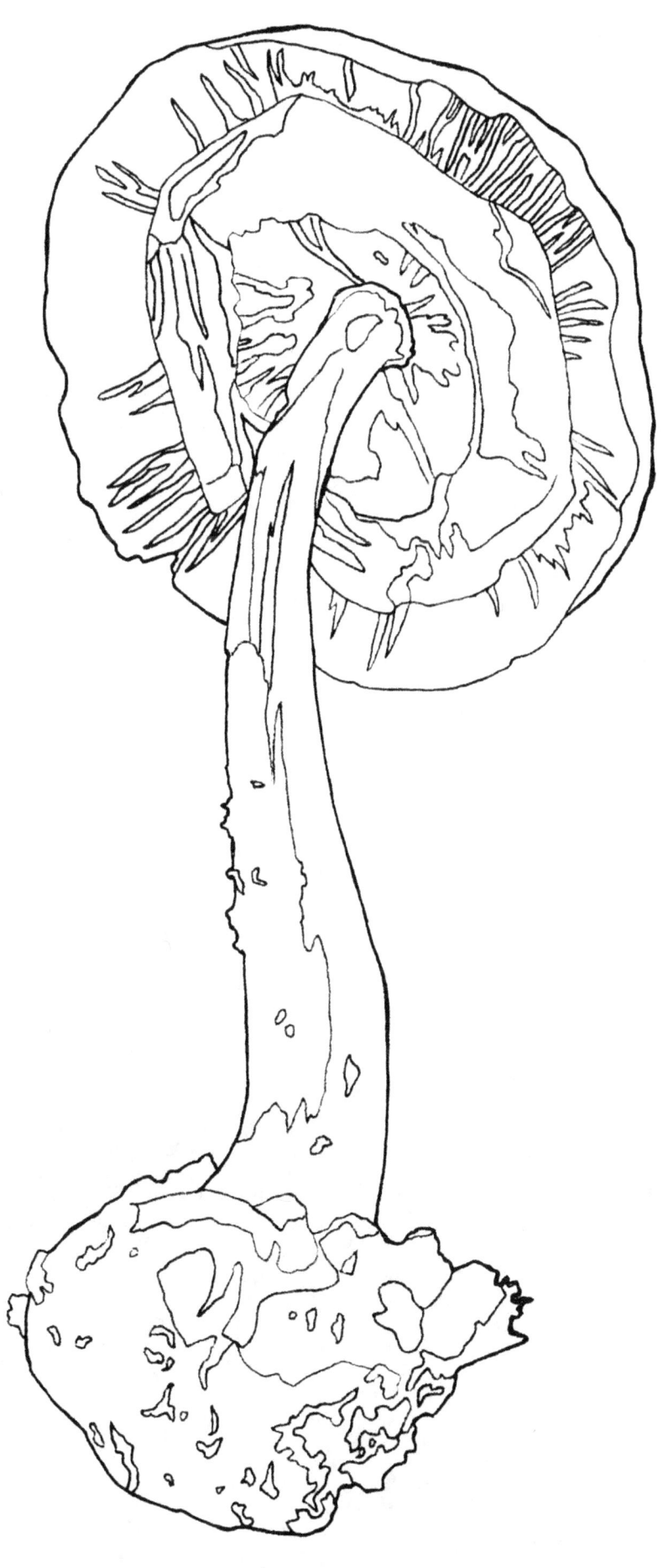

AMANITA BISPORIGERA, DESTROYING ANGEL

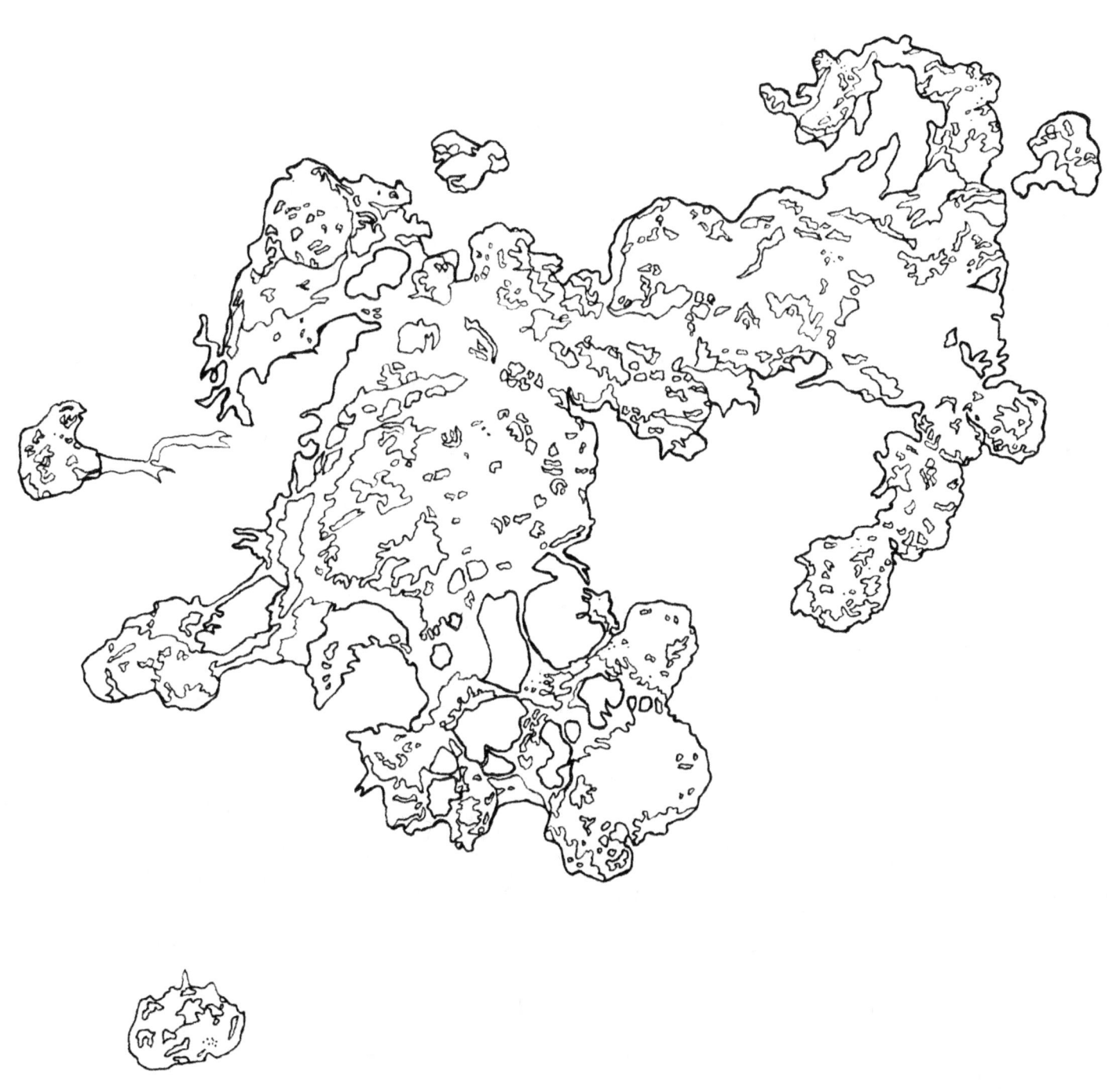

FULIGO, SLIME MOLD

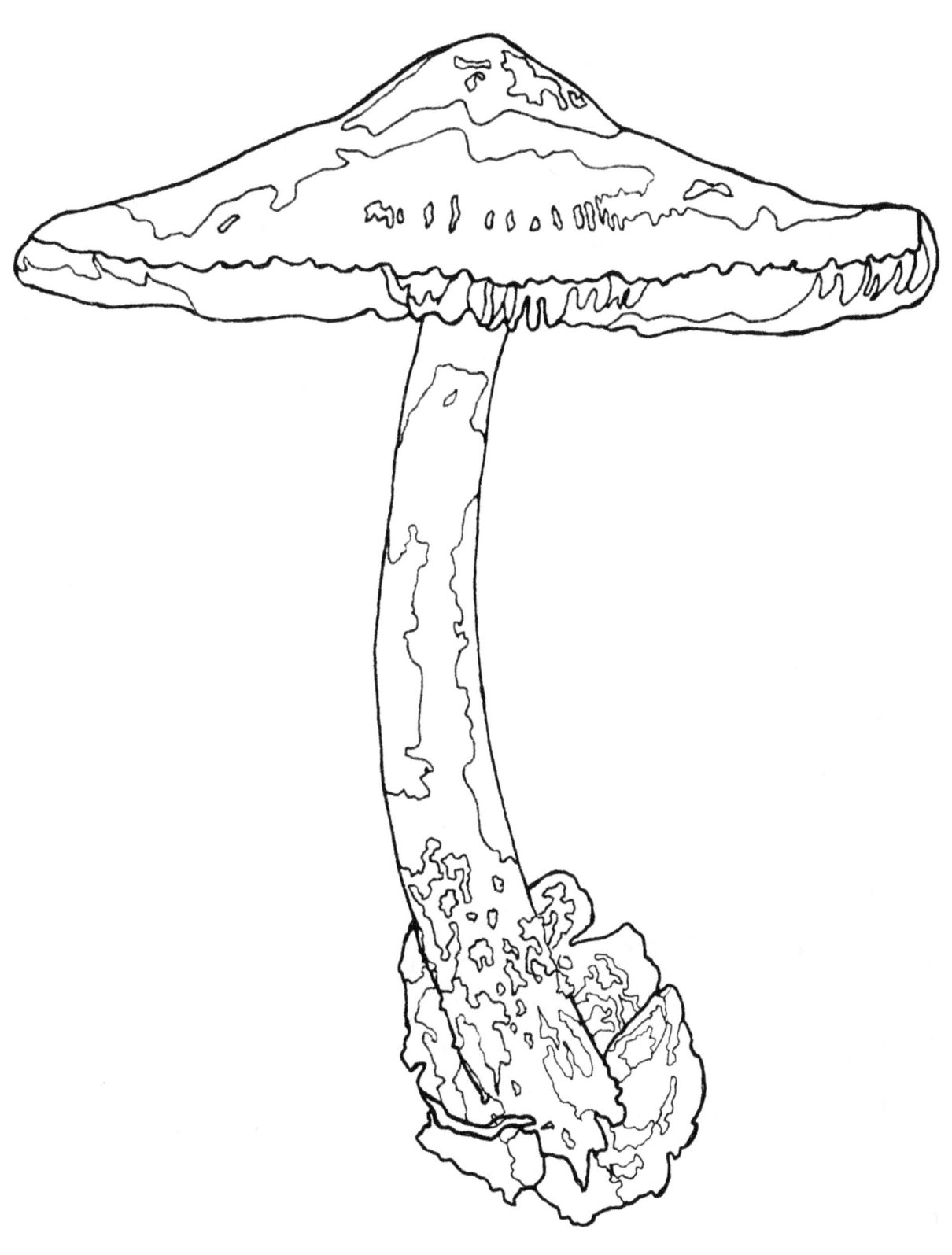

AMANITA VAGINATAE

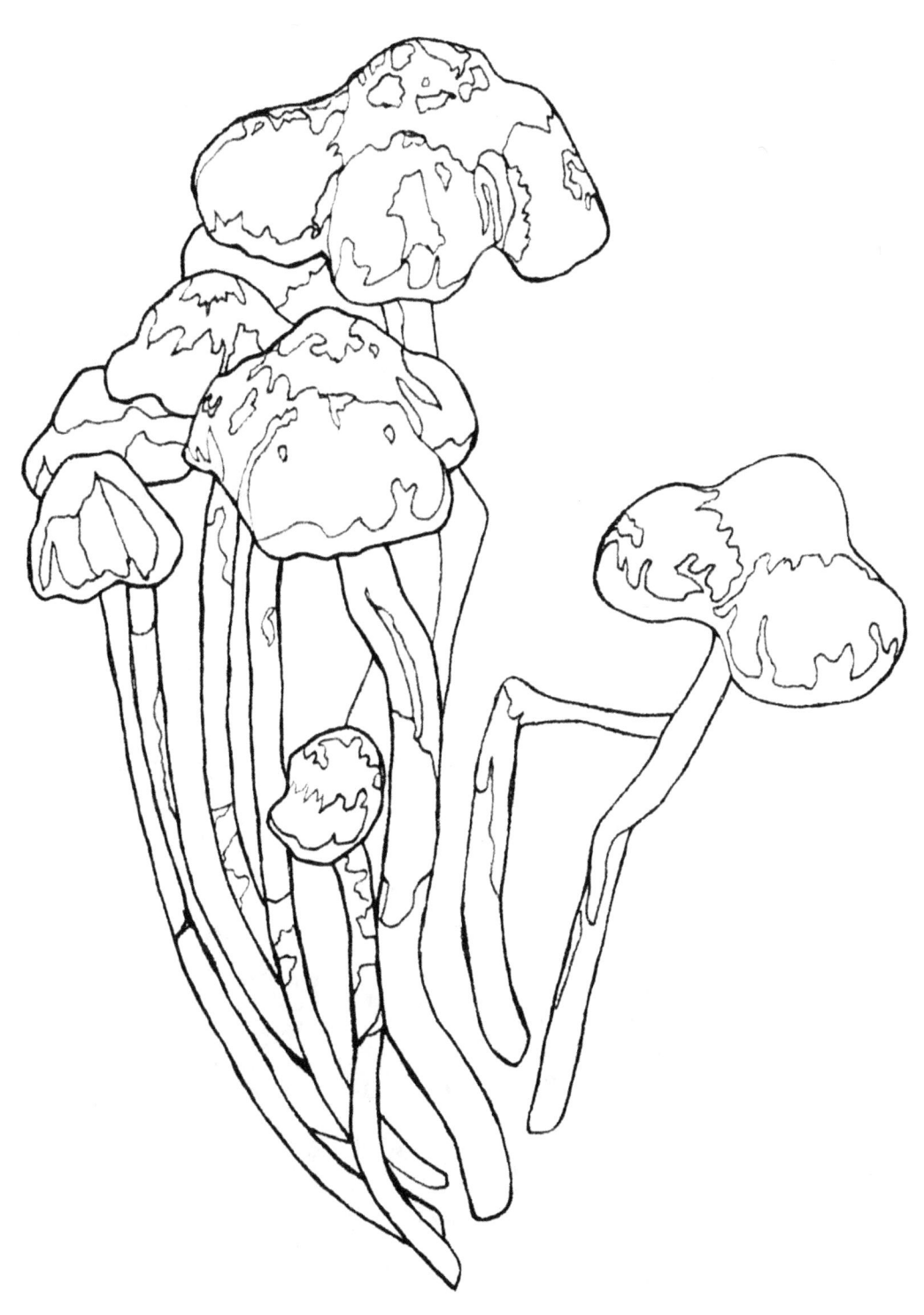

MARASMIUS COHAERENS

GYMNOPILUS

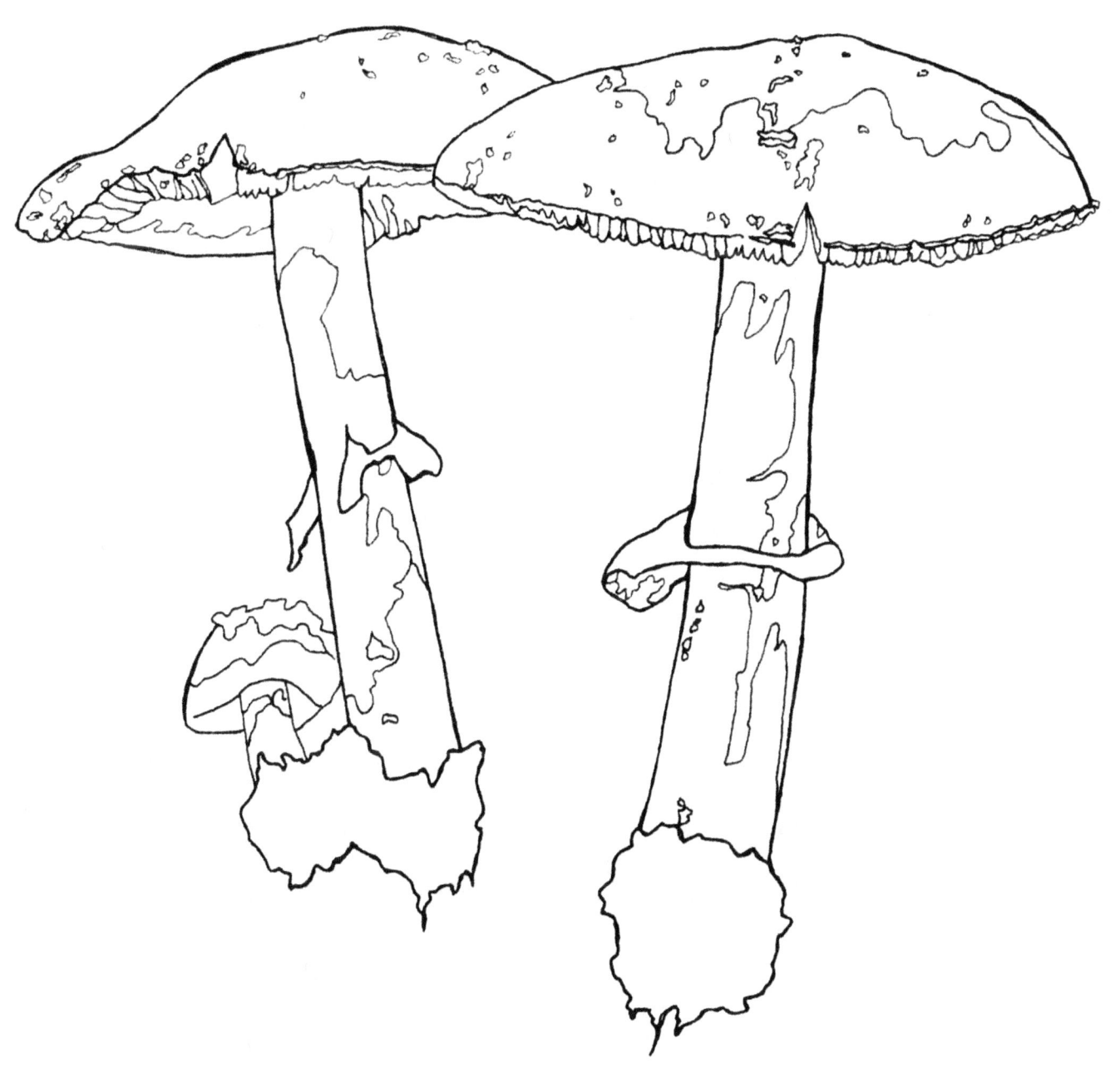

AMANITA VALIDAE

FOMITOPSIS PINICOLA

CLADONIA CHLOROPHAEA, PIXIE CUP LICHEN

ARMILLARIA TABESCENS

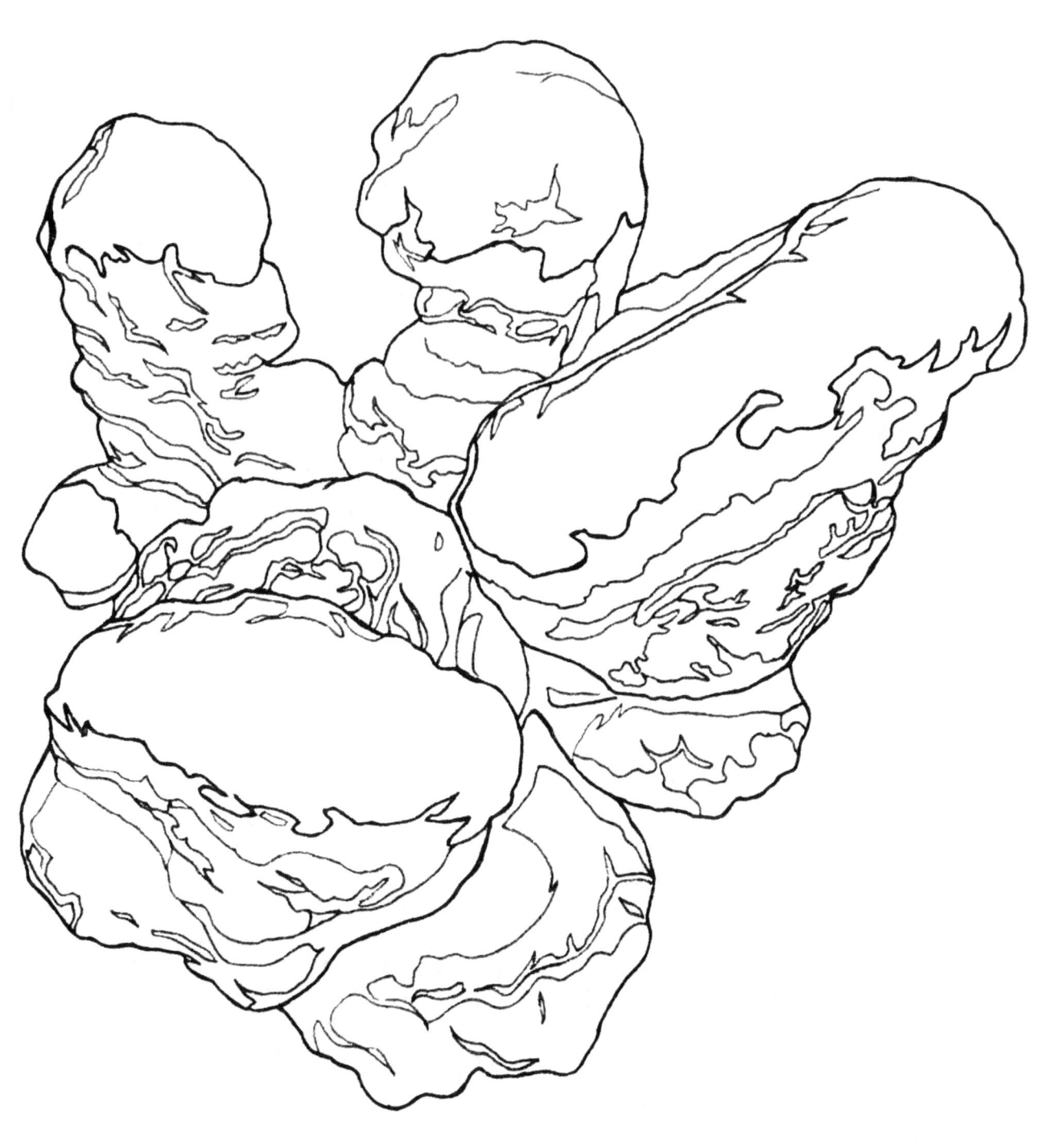

LAETIPORUS, CHICKEN OF THE WOODS

www.ingramcontent.com/pod-product-compliance
Lightning Source LLC
Chambersburg PA
CBHW051950280526
45789CB00009B/3242